IN THE RAIN SHADOW

IN THE RAIN SHADOW

Leland Kinsey

University Press of New England

HANOVER AND LONDON

Published by University Press of New England,
One Court Street, Lebanon, NH 03766
www.upne.com
© 2004 by Leland Kinsey
Printed in the United States of America
5 4 3 2 1

LIBRARY OF CONGRESS CATALOGING-IN-PUBLICATION DATA
Kinsey, Leland.
In the rain shadow / Leland Kinsey.
    p.   cm.
ISBN 1–58465–440–6 (cloth : alk. paper)—ISBN 1–58465–441–4 (pbk. : alk. paper)
1. Africa—Poetry. I. Title.
PS3561.I573715 2004
811'.54—dc22   2004012150

ACKNOWLEDGMENTS

"Orange Benediction" and "Termites" first appeared in *Matrix*.

I wish to thank Howard Mosher for his hard work in bringing this book to be.

CONTENTS

IN THE RAIN SHADOW

My Cousin in Tanzania

He arrived by way of university,
by way of maize and pepper fields
in central Mexico, where he felt,
if not a failure, insufficient,
by way of growing up a hardscrabble
farmer's son in Vermont.
He arrived in the town of Tukuyu
in the Kipengere Range north of Lake Malawi,
at one of three large state dairy farms
to teach and do what his degree
had taught him. He was assigned one barn
with nine hundred cows.
One hundred thirty-eight pregnant heifers
were shipped over with him.
As they freshened they began to die.
Even before some freshened
they would lie down in wadis,
animal wallows, depressions,
and if found refuse to rise
even if prodded, tail-twisted.
Pied crows often found them first
and pecked out their living eyes,
consumed their vulvas. Many lacked
the strength to deliver calves.
One third died, almost as many calves.
The people of the farm were unable
to help or diagnose.
                    Years later
at a conference he learned
the cattle had suffered from edema
brought on by altitude. The farm lay
on an eight-thousand-foot-high plateau.
He had often walked down the long slope

to the tropics on days off or market days,
and returned breathing hard
but never thought of that.
                        The aid project
he worked for persisted with state sanctioned farms
too long, found that the good
did not work down to farmers, villages.

After five years he moved north to Arusha
to head the entire country's dairy project.
He had married in Mbeya, honeymooned
under the Livingston Mountains, took his Swiss-
German wife from her third-generation holdings.
He knew every farmer under contract then.
Wrote the contract himself requiring
every recipient to pass the first calf back
to each area program for redistribution,
each dairy cow a holding not a gift.
New contracts require first and third calves,
yet each animal affords an immediate
prospering in health and goods acquired.
And now beyond heifers: goats, and water buffalo,
chickens, and hares, bees, dairy camels.
and fish for farming after the long rains.
Eight thousand contracts now, and he knows
mostly each program's elected supervisor,
sees them mostly once a year, unless there's trouble.
Some do not enforce zero-grazing rules;
free-range their own cattle; distribute passover
calves outside the rules; abuse vehicle rights
or the vehicles themselves in a land
where walking is the norm. My cousin visits
troubled programs, meets with each council
as arbiter and suggester, his only power—
to award no more contracts. "Kinsey!"
he is called everywhere he goes,

everywhere I went with him.
Farmers' co-ops, women's groups, dioceses,
because they are organized often act
as program grantees. Even the churches can't
discriminate, one Muslim upon receiving
a cow from a Lutheran program
named it *I would not have believed.*
My cousin wrote a *book* on dairy management,
which has been translated into Chinese,
and is often quoted. "I hear 'Kinsey says,'
and 'Kinsey says,'" one woman said,
"and I am glad to meet you among us."
Visiting a farmer who lives on the shoulder
of Kilimanjaro—near where, in the early years
of his twenty in Africa, my cousin could still catch
stocked German brown trout in cold streams
like those of his homeland--she told him,
"My cows are dying, my fodder is poor,
it is too bad for you to see this." He spoke sharply
to her. "You should have called your supervisor.
You must not wait for me." But as we toured
her barns and grounds, the cows were fat,
the fodder plentiful, she even had a biogas
plant to give her clean cooking gas
and one steady bright light her children
did their homework late by.
"We caught her with her pants down,"
he said. "Then she realized she was alright."
"Kinsey!" one man said, "I must make trouble
so I can see you more often."
"He runs his programs perfectly,"
my cousin said, "good training,
a para-vet program with good follow-up
on healthy cattle and practices."
Ordering breakfast one day in our travels—
I had millet porridge, thick and grey

so they call it mercury—the waiter
said to my cousin, "You speak Swahili
better than me."

My cousin drives, flies, boats, bikes, hikes,
traversing the country
from the islands of Pemba and Mafia
in the Indian Ocean, to Ukarere
in Lake Victoria. From the high plateaus
of the interior, to the tsetse fly infested
lowlands, though those are mostly
set aside as national parks—wild animals adapted
long ago to bites a human dies from.
Dairy cattle die from sleeping sickness,
east coast fever, rinderpest, hemorrhagic septicemia,
black quarter, anthrax, foot and mouth.
For those and others he must make inoculations
and care part of every program, push it hard.
He travels to outbreaks to help and reassure.
And he must sit in offices and bargain
for dollars from agents of agencies
who face many clamoring hands.
He dedicates and allocates what he has
and hopes to have; always must scale
back and disappoint. He has appointed
regional heads and gives them their heads.
"Part of my job is to work myself
out of a job. To know the difference
between the worker and the work."

Before the Long Rains

yet long after they should have come
to this part of Africa,
the sultriness becomes an overcast
of deep grey-red whose dust will not be washed
out or settled by the wished for
slashing relief.
The days begin with alto-stratus,
cumulus, but all clouds dissipate by noon.
occasional distant virga tantalizes,
as does one morning's snow on Mt. Meru.
Such reports made the first explorers
sound like sun-baked fools.
The snow looks like hoarfrost
on a late autumn day in Vermont.
Wind and equatorial sun will sublime
most of this sublime cover,
melt providing some relief
only meters lower than its fall.
The green belt on the mountain slopes
does not even reach the base
of parched fields and dry savannah.
As if plant could be expectant,
blooming by heritage to advantage
their seeds, a flowering occurs
in deepest drought—**cassia trees**
in several colors, **tulip trees, jacaranda**
in the year's second blooming, **coral trees,**
flame trees, and **flamboyant,**
extravagant blossoms like shocked-open mangoes,
bottle brush trees though no water
for them or washing. Shrubs too—**frangipani,**
moon flower, a morning glory whose white moons
writhe close to the moonscape earth; gaudiest of all.

bougainvilleas in all colors and arrays
by wrought iron gates and mansion garden
and farmer's lane and elementary bower.
Many of these plants were hand carried
from South America,
plants that sustain only vision
now wild to flower,
spread their seed,
growing for their own purposes.

The farmers are turning to dusty fields,
turning fields to dust, with mattock, ox plow,
gang plows behind desperate tractors.
They always want the fields set
before the rains, no working them
once they're wet, giving the seeds
the chance to grow and set
for full fruiting when the rains end.
If they end in time. If they begin.
The farmers turn from the present and the past
with the prayer to the future work makes,
the silent plea of sowing.

Getting There

Out of the crowded streets of Nairobi
we picked up speed to the south,
heading for the border.
Being my first time in-country
I sat behind the driver
not knowing we would never
do less than one hundred forty kilometers
an hour except at traffic controls
and military roadblocks, which I could tell
from the Indian man in the back
were not reliably legal
as he nervously squirted water
from his bottle to his mouth
after each stop, and offered it to me.
The safari arranger behind me
sat straight, did not watch the terrain.
Wild asses and zebras grazed
in the greener margins
of the narrow paved highway,
sometimes crossing far ahead.
Ostriches raced through the shrubby
dusty flatlands, often seeming
about to cut in front of us.
After the long stop
at the border, with its beggars,
and sellers of food and selves,
the hands at your pockets and packs,
the long looks of officials,
we were up to speed again.
Bicyclists were honked off the road,
slow lorries were passed on straights
or long curves without knowing
who or what might arrive right before us.

The irreducible black and bright pigment
of the thousands of superb starlings
as they flew up just at out arrival at
and immediate departure from that moment
and minute place, then the next, and next.
Hours at that speed later
mountain bases and bulks rose
to the south and east, summits lost
in rainless clouds.
                      The last body of water
I'd seen was Lake Turkana in northern Kenya
from thirty-thousand feet just as the jet began
its long descent over twisted up-thrust mountains
which thrust up swirling winds, buffeting
the whole approach into Nairobi. No rivers
or even streams were extent from there,
only dry wadis, bridges over dust.
                              The city
of our stopping seemed to roll
toward us, to fling us about
with its speed bumps barely slowed for.
We stopped at a high-priced hotel
where I was to meet my cousin
and be given a lift to his family's small cottage.
The hotel seemed encased
in every tropical bloom.
The taxi bus stopped, I got out
on wobbly legs, good and transported.

Lushoro

Biking up a sandy road,
still washboard from the short rains
two months ago, and hedged
by a fine-leaved shrub,
    the underside of each leaflet
    of which was heavily barbed,
    named, in translation from Swahili, *wait a while,*
I tired quickly from the pitch
of road and afternoon sun.
My cousin, his three sons, and I entered
the yard of a farmer my cousin knew,
and sat on worn plank benches
beneath a large Australian oak.
We could look back down the steep shoulder
of Mount Meru to the busy Old Nairobi Road,
or at least the hedge of dust
that rose between the hedges.
The farmer insisted we drink
and brought us metal cups
cool with condensation.
"*Lushoro,*" my cousin said
and drank large drafts.
I tipped my cup and tasted
sour milk with curds solid enough
to chew, and looked to see
a greyish whey with hulled corn
at the bottom. My cousin was now spooning
out of this like a fountain float.
I tipped and chewed some corn
for a hard swallow.

As a child I had drunk a cup
of vinegar-soured cream
in my mother's pantry,
large acidic lumps sliding down
and right back up over jars and cans
and flour tub—my mother's
punishment twice mine
though mine was harsh.

I sat in the shade long
finishing my treat, bad etiquette
to leave generosity half gone.
Biking on, my cousin
did not make it worse
or better by telling me
that *lushoro* is made in gourds
washed with cattle urine,
a quite sterile fluid, then cauterized
with a hot coal. Milk, hominy,
a mildly antibiotic plant
to prevent the souring going too far,
are introduced and allowed to work.
The gourds are kept damp
so evaporation cools the preparation
and makes for a soothing drink
if one is used to it.
"People favor this," he said, "get used to it.
It will be offered often,
at times the only drink." It was.
I did not ever like the taste,
but could drink the whey
and clotted smoothness down to the maize
for a thorough chew without a flinch.
In a land where people starve,
no compliment to me.
My stomach almost always ached
depending on how much the drink had worked.

Late that day I hit a sand patch, clumsily fell
and rasped open my face, bare arm,
and both hands on the hedge,
painful in entanglement,
lovely in the offering.

In the Rain Shadow of Mount Meru

Young camels' groaning calls
carry to their mothers
far off in the acacia wooded valley.
Dead acacia bushes, branches, trees,
dragged to corral the young so the mothers must
at day's end come to hunger made loud.
The largest of the three camel varieties
stand taller, walk like white-sand greatbeasts
among the savannah camels,
move high as trucks
through acacia, along passages
carved out by lesser kudus
where it seems a slipped-in page might tear.
The least of the camels produce more milk
than an average cross-bred cow. ,

Quiet hunger resides higher
up the hillside in a Maasai *shamba*.
All the daub and wattle huts,
network of beaten cedar strips
plastered with mud and dung,
sit inside the acacia *kraal* for protection
from predators, mostly gone now,
marauding elephants, and enemy warriors, also gone,
all who slank into the history of landscape.
Women and children disappeared quickly
at our approach, reappeared suddenly
and as completely as the two crane-legged sentinels
draped in red cloth, leaning on their staffs.
They stood at one of the four gates,
which by accident or intent lay
in the cardinal directions,
like portals to some ancient city.

The gates themselves were thorn trees
grey and rounded as driftwood,
except the thorns,
drawn athwart each opening at night.

The landscape plants and earth lay
as brittle in the drought
as the crack-checked walls of huts.
About the compound bright birds
sat like strewn nuggets of turquoise,
and disturbed, rose and settled as if tossed,
cordon bleu and red-cheeked cordon bleu.

One man invited me into his home.
Smoke and its thick residue
on thatch, rafters, upper walls,
choked, and brought aching tears
to my eyes already blinded in his simple
maze of a house which occludes light.
A curved wall and rail divide and include
animal and home. A single birdhouse-hole
opening opposite the door side admits
the only light and little air,
the entire house an efficient damper
for the tiny fire. My cousin lifted the spurtle
from its pot. Its four-pointed star
lowered through milk, blood, millet porridge
by a handle hand smoothed and sweat stained
and sweated of its now ancient sap
to the look and feel of celadon,
stirred thoroughly as I spun it
as if trying to light a fire by ancient means.
The grandmother sat cross-legged
by the twig-and-branch racks like bookshelves
which are their beds, which she offered
to let us rest upon. She offered
room-temperature sodas,

a popular brand there, hot with spice.
I exited, throat stinging from smoke
and ginger beer.
                        Stinging sand
eroded our faces a little,
the land a lot, shortened our vision
before great dust devils
swirled aloft and off on winds
dried and falling from the mountain.
The mountain from this side was a pyramid,
from the other, lopsided crater and ash cone
where it had blown a top higher than Kili
wide on the landscape. Winds from the ocean
rose along the crater side
and dropped moisture from the cooled updraft
on the downwind slope and left
the land northwest cast
in a long rain shadow. Those dried
and drying winds, dry as the ash clouds
that fell long past, ran falling fast
out onto the vast bush lands, a taxonomist's
dream of thorn trees:
whistling acacias, whose ant-emptied galls
catch the constant wind in the drilled holes
to produce the notes they're named for,
carried a note as distant as hearing;
scissor acacia, whose crossed thorns
will entangle and hold fast
to skin and clothes should you fall in,
only another's assistance will extract you;
hexagon acacia, forming joints of twig and thorn
at sixty degrees, made me feel like a student
looking at replicas of molecules,
a geometric shade of life's construct;
and acacia with thorns like railroad spikes
that no foot or tire can resist,
no mouth can crush. All but the last

are simply a menu for the camels,
leather-mouthed like their giraffe cousins.
The pale Somali camels stood above the bush
the rest of the herd moved among,
grazing far down the valley
where the higher water table kept leaves greener.

The Maasai had watched the camels
survive the drought, where cattle could not.
Their cattle died of thirst if not moved to market,
a market where what was offered was a tithe of worth.
They had heard the camels would be theirs in time.
How long a time, they asked, and how.
Training must come first, my cousin said,
Camels are much like cattle, and much different.
Here was a people whose language, developed
long before their prehistoric exile here,
was agrarian based, with words for farming
and its methods, who now denigrated anyone but herders.
Cattle herders. The Somali man who had helped
assemble the herd and bring it south
through the wilds of Kenya said,
A man who raises camels is a man,
who raises goats is half a man,
who raises cattle is no man at all.
Crossed visions, yet the Maasai seemed
to hope the be-all of a tenuous future
was the camel, foraging native plants
that have become thick with the lack of feeders,
walking spread-footed on the baked soil,
drinking and conserving water
with their thick urine.
                          The Somali intoned
often that people should come to heal
themselves. One week drinking camel milk
will cure any disease he said, and if not, then ...
he peeled a strip of dried urine,

the color and consistency of dried blood,
where it had dribbled down the rear leg of one camel,
and chewed it. That would, he said, cure absolutely.

A few days before my arrival he had hurried
his best camel twenty kilometers to Arusha
to race against imported camels in an exhibition.
His tall, long-legged camel easily won
over the ten-kilometer course
starting and ending at the track
where colonial thoroughbreds
had once raced in the cool season.
He returned the distance back
to camp by evening.
                    Some of the camels
were recovering from being kept
in water-rationed Namanga without water
for almost a month. All survived,
a testament arising from bad management.

We waited in the evening for the herd
to return. Out of the acacia curtain
they assembled themselves, a riderless
caravan coming home. Dairy camels
do not spit or bite, I could reach up
yet not reach the chins of some,
but they would lower their heads
even on my shoulder if I let them.
The left cheeks lowered to my cheek
had knife-slice scar brands
of various design.

The white man who has brought
the camels here is the son
of the dislodged former owner.
He remembers the flight for their lives.
They had controlled one hundred thousand

acres, villages and all.
What was their house sits on a high shoulder
of the mountain, visible from camel camp
but two thousand feet higher.
A pleasant climate he assured us,
where officers of the district reside.
We sat in heat
like a volcano's breath.
Even the birds were parched.
My cousin poured a little water
into a bowl-like stone.
The plashy sound alone brought some,
in half an hour twenty species
had swept in, straw-tailed wydahs,
barbets, bishop birds, scrub robins,
masked weavers, purple grenadiers,
all brilliant darts in the ochre landscape.
The father dreamed of bringing camels
to the Maasai. He had also searched the horn
and into Arabia for natural cottons,
a long staple cotton for their cloth,
wanting to settle a nomadic people.
He said the crops helped the people
but his huge farm had also prospered.
The son was denied reentry for a time,
a fear he wanted the land back.
He longs to set up camel farms
on a large scale here and farther south,
to ride the camels even to Namibia.
My cousin wants the people to learn
by owning, believes fewer camels will die,
not more as the man worries, that better care
will be taken one on one.

Working our way in to the camel camp,
negotiating roads we almost needed
treads to follow, we picked up

two girls with heavy burdens.
One was urban dressed,
a runaway my cousin guessed
from the story she told,
trying to get back to her people.
The other had never ventured far
from the village, her body draped
in bright native cloth in some volume.
She had never ridden in a motor vehicle,
the urban girl said and laughed
as she rattled on about cities and men.
The village girl crouched behind the seat,
daring to peek up and out only rarely,
yelping at the bumps and steep pitches.
She cried as she scrambled out
when we met her brother by the track
with his herd of goats.
I scanned the landscape with binoculars
trying to find the camels. He motioned
if he could look. I passed the glasses over,
and he jumped back from the lenses
when Kili, fifty miles away,
seemed right in front of him, its ice
bright enough to make eyes ache.
He and his sister had never been
even the ten miles to the highway.
The greater world was coming fast
to fill their view, but would be hard
to reach, and all of it a dangerous journey.

Ownership of the camels would pass.
The arid, hoof-torn grasslands may revive
so what few wild beasts survive
will have food, if small chance
against poachers and long hunger.

In this place and time of vexation and drift
the camels may be one curative,
source of milk, blood, meat
in the long trek towards what comes next.

A Southern Sky

Under Polaris all my life
I felt misplaced without it above me.
Only the flanks of Ursa Major
rose over the horizon,
bobtailed at last.

Carina, ship of ancient cultures
including the marine Swahili,
sailed high above the distant skyline,
its massive Eta in a roil
of destruction, colorfully blowing
layers of itself away
brighter than ten thousand suns,
but below naked-eye visibility now.
I found it with binoculars.

Sun poured into the bus
west of Lake Victoria
where ironworks from twenty-five hundred B.P.E.,
though crumbled, stand.
Told I taught astronomy,
a man asked, "What is the sun made of?"
Wondrous to answer
a basic question promptly.
"Hydrogen. It's fusing into helium
in the middle. Like an H-bomb
the size of several oil tankers
blowing every second."
The man smiled and shook his head.
I thought of the flux of iron
at a furnace core, the forger's genius.
The sun poured

in the windows with the heated wind.
Melting seemed a possibility.

One night at camel camp
I glassed the Megellanic Clouds.
That they might bring the needed monsoon
seemed as possible as real clouds
occulting the sky.
I showed those
and Mars and a globular cluster
to agricultural interns, told them
the cluster might have a million stars
like our sun, and that the Clouds
were islands of stars beyond
our own galaxy, the path-like band.
I tried to describe distance,
and watched that between us
grow and shrink in odd ways.
"Do little men come?
We have heard of these."
I laughed, "No, but planets revolve
around some stars, maybe life,
but it hasn't been here."
I scanned Crow and the Southern Cross,
both novelties to me.
A faint, short rain of meteors
seemed bright. I said, "The Earth picks up
thousands of tons of dust each year."
"We don't need dust," said one.
Another, "We speak of the stars
as grains of millet. That looked like threshing."

Like cowboys in the American West
kept track of night watches,
I timed our standing by the counterclockwise
rise and turn of Ursa Major's tail.

Our faces were animated,
craned back, lit by starlight;
our voices, quick with excitement,
spoke of and questioned
each new image and gleaning
as we moved through the Milky Way.

Village Furrow

A neighbor has pleached her mulberry bushes
as hedge and for heavy fruiting,
and they and her citrus grove are parched.
She waits, out at three in the morning,
for her allotted hours of flooding
from the village furrow.
The water is cold
outflow from yesterday's snow
at the mountain's peak
that puts its downwind slope
in rain shadow.
Channeled from the Blood River,
site of a battle two hundred years ago
where the victors hacked the defeated captives
apart in the river that then ran red,
the furrow's small deep flow
is parted out. Each shareholder
is allowed a semi-monthly inundation
of till land. Machete-bearing
guards are necessary, especially at night
when hijacking of the flow is common.
From so steep a rush the slowing spread
drops rich black silt
on doughty soil. I hear the rasp
of hoes as the dikes are breached,
the small dry breeze
brings the smell of wetted soil
like evaporating rain on a hot day.
The water flows softly,
carefully channeled to sink not run.
Where the furrow runs by the road
further down in front of small shops,
the keepers are out in the early morning

tossing unpaid-for cups of the water
onto the road to settle the dust
for part of the day.

Two rivers that run
through the town are down
to the size of large furrows.
Safari outfitters drive their vehicles
into the remaining pools to clean them,
tourists demand polish so the grime
is washed downstream, to salt lakes
in the interior.
                    In the plots
irrigation must be complete
so the soil salts are not drawn out
to concentrate in the thin arable surface.
The neighbor's furrow dikes
are closed, and the clatter of tools
carried tiredly home precedes the workers,
only the land skirmished with.
The diminished furrow proceeds
to the next inundation.

Junk Toys

In the jam of congested alleys
and on the paths in remote bush lands
I noticed African children race home-built toys.
Push-toys with long handles for steering
made from bleach and detergent bottles,
indestructible for use or as refuse,
ingeniously cut and hinged to imitate long-haul freighters,
or piped with windows like the high-wheeled overland buses.
All rode wooden or plastic cap wheels
of disproportionate size like the real
which must straddle and overcome
the swamps and ranges called roads.

Some toy buses for market, made of wood scraps,
wire for working springs,
and pounded out tin can sides
cut and painted the white and blue
of the national transport company,
reminded me of our local failing general store
where the only work the husband performed
was cutting and carving models,
from busted nail kegs, fruit crates, cigar boxes,
of carriages and wagons such as his elders
employed. Sometimes he would place them out
on garden poles to no known end but ruin.
Mostly he hung them about the store for outsiders.
He would point to them as his industry,
talk of sales, and overprice them for our longing.

Such fidelity for tourists rules south of here
in dusty alleys and under dry-wash bridges
and the porticos and plazas of colonial *bomas,*
as bicycles and tricycles

and wagons and oxen take form from cast off wire
in the hands of practiced street children.
Hand-held perfection in shape and workings,
souvenirs but seldom toys.

But in this land, country or city,
children trundled their caravans of recycled
workaday goods made truly plastic,
form, and form of, play.

The Golden Farmer

A farmer was honored today,
five hundred miles of terracing
in thirty-five years of labor
for his village. He is shy.
His wife asked her company in to eat
before my cousin and his wife drove
the couple to the ceremony. They offered us
boiled goat, plantains, *lushoro,*
a variety of sodas—safer
and easier than tea or coffee
for which water would be carted long.
His daughter circled the table
to pour a fine stream of water
over our hands. She caught it
in a basin held under our hands
as we quickly scrubbed. Out of the common pot
we each drew pieces recognizable
or not, and ate it down to skeleton.
When all were done, the daughter
circled once again, this time with soap.
They took us to the kitchen garden
that the grey water waters, a small bottle
inverted by each plant.
He showed us his fruit orchard
for the family and for sale,
and his stand of legume trees
to feed his cattle constantly penned
so they cannot ruin the ground
with their hooves and browsing.
The trip to the village was up
from his high farm. The hills are ringed
like topographic lines, lines of trees,
shrubs, elephant grass hold the taller

outer part of each great step
the gold farmer has helped devise.

Every church pew, every school desk
had been taken from the tamped
dirt floors and set out in rows
on the promontory common.
Wattle-and-daub houses with thick thatch roofs
surround the common,
as do the tops of surrounding hills.
A double line of women marched
from the church, their voices raised
in multi-parted exaltation.
Large beaded rings around their necks
moved in sinewy rhythm
as they shrugged their shoulders in unison
to the chanted hymns.
A speech from the sector agricultural chief,
then one in English and Swahili
from my cousin, who had taught
the farmer new surveying methods
better and faster than chain and rod.
The farmer was given a goat as prize.
My cousin was given a stool
carved from a single block of ebony,
a bark-cloth vest,
and an elder's staff smoothed
by hand with shards of glass.
Depending on how presented,
narrow or bulbous end foremost,
the knobkerrie signals peace, or war.

Returning the farmer and wife home
we saw hoopoes by the hedgerows,
striped mongooses in the margins.
The farmer's children had hung a *cutting cane*
large rat named as verb not noun,

for sale on a stick by the road.
The children protect the pearl millet,
thatch is made from the long fat stems,
cattail-like heads hulled for grain.
The rat harvest also pays as local protein.
In a poor land, wealth lies in these details.

African Barrows

Fathers, uncles, grandfathers in Vermont
built carts and trailers from the disused
parts of pickups, cars,
the frames and axles, spindles, drums,
with dented mismatched wheels
and balding, often bulging tires,
to pull behind our trucks and tractors
to carry such loads as they could.

In this land such barrows are pushed
or pulled by one, two, or three men
as needed, as incline and load demand.
Ungreased bearings often squawk;
wheels often made of cast concrete
because cement is cheap.
Truck horns sound their way around
the slow and awkward. The cart haulers
are silent but for the slap of tire-tread sandals.
Most of the urban burden is foot sped—
cement in bags and blocks; milk cans
from the immediate country; carvings,
large and small; sundries for crate-sized stores
that line back streets and dusty byways;
long poles and beams for construction;
grain bags piled high, corn and millet
for cattle feed or breweries.
But the finished millet beer
is lucrative, trucks transport it
to bars the haulers throng to.
The musky smell fills streets
and mouths, bacteria-free substance.

My father once drove an overladen
homemade trailer up a barn's highdrive,
had to back it up twice to draw it in.
My uncle came behind grim and smiling.
"Pull a little hard? You left the axle
on the ramp." A day's necessary work done.

Sometimes here collapse of overdeveloped lungs
or an enlarged heart's failure
leaves body and load stranded roadside.
Near relatives will often come,
more distant ones might not.
Carted home or to a resting place,
the final exchange occurs, the barrow pushed through life
for the mounded rock-crowned barrow,
the whole burden of earth.

Pit Sawyers

Beside the road I climbed
on the verdant shoulder of Meru,
three men had dug
a pit the size and depth
of two graves put side to side.

They said they had come east
from Kagere, renowned for its lumbermen
the house builder said, who had hired
these men to cut timber for his home and shop.
He translated that too many sawyers
worked back home, and no one to buy
the lumber sawn.

They had slabbed off one side
of a stout oak log one meter through
and three long. It sat athwart
the pit on two bent boles
of slender trees bearing this great one.
Having rolled the slabbed side uppermost,
they'd snapped lines on it with an ashy cord.
Half the first long rip had been accomplished
when I came up and they quit for a smoke.
The top sawyer walked his sap-wet
post like a captain on deck for show.

Other houses along the way
were beamed and sided with planks
and boards with obvious saw marks
of the hand done, the same almost-straightness.
This unlike the work of shipbuilders
when the curves of wood members had to be right,
when only a sawyer and his pitman

could create and follow the necessary lines.
I thought of a foundation to a vertical sawmill
which stands by a brook on my uncle's land.
The timbers and sheathing for his aged barns
were sawn there. No sufficient steady flow
exists here to create such a thing.
No modern machine will run at such low cost
as these men have bid down to.
Because the wood was sawed for ease,
the least depth in the long rips,
and not to the grain, warping would twist
the boards in time, and structures with them.
Older houses, stores, barns canted,
curled up or down at corner and end,
kissed supporting trees.

The three went back to it.
The top man pulled the broad guide end,
almost two feet wide, the bottom man
pulled the narrow end
and all the sawdust toward him.
What was for me an uplift of exotic smell
must sometimes stifle almost as much
as the constant drawing from the kerf.

Along most of the blade's length, at least half
had been sharpened away.
The sawyer had set the wide triangle teeth
to bite both sides of the kerf
he bestrode with bare feet
inches from the bright filed edges.
He had all his toes but said relations
had severed several pieces and parts.

It took three men to shift the log
when they came to cross pieces;
and the third spelled the pitman.

Both tramped the sawdust damp with sweat
as they halved the log, quartered it, and down,
making the pit less hot and dangerous,
thinning the oppression of the draw.

The Night Guards

The guards arrived as silent as the sunset.
At the end of the day's heat
they arrive swaddled for the night's cold.
Each of the two stands in turn at the door;
coffee in a thermos, bread and cheese,
from the goats they also guard,
yogurt, and fruit are handed out. They favor apples,
hard and green—all that will grow
in the Pare Mountains, planted
by Germans fleeing the summer,
orchards later tended by the English—
because they never had them
before this work. Sometimes as I lay
awake late, I heard the soft crunch
as though from home. I also heard
the pad, pad, pant, pant of the dogs,
an Alsatian and a Ridgeback,
the latter a lion dog which would section
an intruder out.
                    Before they had guards,
my cousin and his wife were forced
by robbers into the kitchen while their boys
lay asleep. Threatened with death,
forced to lie down on the stone floor
and give up some of their secrets,
they thought a curtain came down
when they prayed. It upset me
that they thought a Lord so picayune.
One might better say the men's humanity
kept them from killing.

After surgery in hospital in Nairobi,
my cousin's wife lay in a friend's house
when thieves pulled up roof tiles
and came through the ceiling.
They beat her in her bed
in surprise at a guest being
where they had expected absence.

After the father-in-law's death,
thieves overcame the mother-in-law's single guard
and entered her home, broke
her arm, displaced her hip,
left her bloodied as they fled
with her goods.

The guards sit in the dark
in the greater shadows on the bench
inside the gate, machetes across
their knees, or walk the garden fence
beyond the double bird-of-paradise,
the roses from long-ago Europe—
regrown from cuttings each family move—
over the edge of the huge termite mound,
along the goat and rabbit pens—
to the thunk of hooves on slats
and the slap of paws—back to sitting
for another essential coffee
as they look carefully down
the streetlightless crowded street,
which a decade ago was a rural part of town.

My choice was rest under my mosquito net,
or wakefulness at the window,
as I looked up into a brilliant black sky
and listened to the soft stirrings,

and, because the guards were
my dark adjusted eyes
and my protective arms,
needed to be only curious.

At the Gate

The woman with the crippled daughter
waits at the gate. The note the house
guard brings my cousin's wife states
the woman is waiting for her sewing machine.
The woman's husband left a year ago,
to work in the Kilimanjaro coffee fields
he said, but neither money nor man
has come home. My cousin's wife arranged
for her to take sewing courses
so she might work at home
and tend the daughter who is eighteen
and lives a small child's life.
The church voted to donate sixty thousand
Tanzanian shillings, not quite a hundred
dollars, for her to buy a used machine.
Today she must have it,
but the money is not there.
My cousin's wife dips into the offering stash
so the woman might begin
to make some ends meet.

We are washing apples and plums,
small hard fruits that only grow
in the upper valleys of the Pare Mountains.
We wash them in boiled water twice
on the bench outside the door,
and we are called by a man at the gate.
He has heard my cousin's wife is a nurse
and wants her to check his boy's leg
where his foot was accidentally amputated
by a heavy knife three days ago.
The boy was cutting fodder trees
for cattle, his eight-year-old arm

able to wield but not slow
the necessary blade. She walks the mile
up the road to rebandage,
and worries about infection on return.

We sit past supper in the dense sultriness
of night and days before the long rains.
The sunbirds have stopped moving
in the cassia trees, the hornbills'
sharp moaning ended. My cousin talks
of thunderstorms in Vermont, the washed-out roads
and bridges, flattened hayfields. Roads here
are little better in the best of times.
The crops are dying because the long rains are late,
and the short rains of spring, November and December,
failed. The house keeper, chopping
greens, cries from the kitchen,
"The meat teacher is at the gate."
My cousin goes out to bring him in.
The headmaster of the Greek school
has slaughtered today and has brought
goat quarters for the freezer,
a somewhat generous gesture, old animals
with lots of gristle, and two infertile
old rabbit does, as well as beans and beets
from his irrigated garden.
It seems he always brings such gifts
late in the evening, so washing,
and cutting, and wrapping become chores.
He has been drinking, as always,
and talks of how he ripped out
all the landscaping at the school
and had new plants placed and sown
ready for the rains and now his grounds
are sere. He finds his students' performance
almost as disappointing, his long lectures
are poorly attended or attended to.

My cousin's boys are waiting
for their ride to school.
When the German driving this week
comes, he stands at the gate
to ask my cousin to tend his dogs and grounds
the month his family will be gone.
The German grows cut flowers
for the European trade and with no rain
the fields he cannot irrigate
will not produce in time,
nor will the flowers grown for seed.
He must move his operations east
toward rain. In addition to the care,
he says be prepared because many of the workers
will appear at his gate worried
about the date or truth of his return.

While grinding coffee one early morning
in the *banda*, an open, vine-shrouded shed,
I noticed suddenly half a man upright
by the gate. He said nothing nor moved
but waited my eye, and when he caught it
moved his hand as if to whisper secrets.
The wheeled board that held his remnant
lower half was hidden by filigree
at the gate's lower edge. "I have been
here before," he said in workable English,
"might you give me something before I must
ask them. The buses are not running
and I must pay extra for a jerry-cab."
I gave him all my change. "Sufficient
unto the day . . . ," I quoted to myself
as he rode away, the small wheels on gravel
sounded like the crush of beans in gears.

The woman with the hydrocephalic baby
did not feel she could wait for day

but stood by the gate and sent
her message in as knocks
and low murmurs by the night guard
at bedroom doors, and we began
the long drive through morning
to the hospital. Three days later
she waited for the light to tell us
the child had not survived,
and might she have a bit,
as from each neighbor,
for the casket.

Coming home from work my cousin was met
at the gate by his wife. A local farmer
had been down twice for aid with a cow
who couldn't give birth. The first time
he had walked the cow the three houses down
to stand at the gate, calf legs protruding
from the heavily breathing cow.
The second time he said she would not rise.
My cousin grabbed some heavy twine
and walked up to find the cow past
saving, but pulled the living calf out.
Training for husbandry was good
but not complete at one go.
No colostrum, no milk even then,
made chances poor, half a day
to barter the calf away or nutrition in.

My cousin's wife weeps sometimes
with all the trials, after decisions
and actions have been taken,
and he is steel-faced
in this iron age of poverty,
though both can sometimes smile at chicanery,
drunks and itinerant beggars with ruses, causes.
Their lives are further flung,

but at this bougainvillea-arbored pass way arrives
the black humor of grief
as well as its plumbed depths,
both of which must be found
to find time and grace,
and a way to grant grace,
for all these recurring entrances,
the eternal exits.

Mother of Vinegar

Mango base, *kapona* too,
double batch fermentations
from rinds and overripe drops,
only one of the waste-not, want-not
products of my cousin's wife's tiny kitchen
in order to make do.
What have become clichés of frugality
at home, staples of my ancestors,
still speak to survival here.
New Englanders' love of vinegar
is no cliché. We eat dandelion greens,
fiddlehead ferns, cucumbers, garden greens,
tomatoes, wild leeks, onions, soaked.
My family even made a potent crude vinegar
by letting bottles of homemade cider
sit in the cellar for months.

She fills the airlock tub with pressings
from the marinated fruit scraps.
She pours last and most carefully
the mother-of-vinegar, reserved
and potent portion of each previous brew,
smell so strong its taste fills the room.
She has small batches processing always
so whatever fruit is ripe—guava, mulberry,
banana, the skins and bits soaked and worked—
comes also to the table soon as vinegar.
Only the variable acidity keeps
her from pickling with the homemade,
for that she buys commercial white.
But after a meal's salads or greens

are gone, my cousin and I vie
to drain the remaining vinegar into a glass
for a drink that leaves
a gloriously sour taste in our mouths.

The Trip Out

My cousin's mother-in-law came out as a girl
on a slow steamer around the cape
because war at the northern horn made the Suez impassable.
Her father had sold his factory in Switzerland
and sailed to grow coffee
in one of the bubble times.
He had to go far inland
to find good land
on the shoulders of the Mybeya Range
north of Lake Nyassa.
The coffee bubble burst
but tea was a crop to make money at,
and the altitude and climate
grew it well on fertile slopes.
House on one side of the valley,
factory on the other.
Managers and tutors were brought
from Europe.
               One tutor
had voyaged out with them, lessons
not to be lost on the weeks at sea.
She remembers the ship's prow
and wake plowing through long calms
and oppressive heat. Even over quiet water
her sister lay seasick for weeks. The captain,
she realizes now, flirted with her mother,
and her father's quiet was deeper
and calmer than the dark seas
they were a film on.

The second man who arrived to manage
the factory was older by ten years
than she, but started courting

with her parents' permission.
Marriage after three years
and a big house on the valley floor
with wide views of the life
and work above in the forested coffee fields,
the bushed tea plantation
stretching up slopes like a topiary sea.

Her father had sold shares
and went back home
to make another fortune
before the war. She had then sailed
a lake each day across to Germany
during her repatriated
higher education,
had seen restrictions, suspicions,
grow. She had begged her way home
early, and wanted to make the long sail
she hated, once again—even longer,
around Good Hope, because of the warring—
out and done, she thought,
with those affairs.
          Many of their friends
in Germany had relatives
who had thought Tanganyika a homeland
before the League of Nations' Mandate.
The colonizers' crimes and cruelties
became not less but pale
for those relatives or returnees,
and thinking of it all
made civility difficult.

Her father sailed them again
to Africa, home of his death;
home of her life's home,
which the thought of ever leaving again
gave her a feeling like illness.

Yogurt

Each day my cousin's wife boils
the goats' milk to make the yogurt
she is locally famous for.
Many pans sit cooling in the kitchen
every morning after she has reduced
and sterilized the day's batch,
then inoculated it with previous yogurt
so her long strain is maintained.
She likes the word *inoculate*
since as a nurse she inoculated
thousands of children and adults
against various diseases
including helping to eradicate
the last pockets of smallpox,
but in this it's aiming toward
an end other than prevention.
She makes the day's deliveries
before shopping for the evening meal.

Her mother made deliveries of yogurt,
feta cheese, and hard ricotta,
at hotels and shops in Umbaya
near Lake Nyassa, both as a girl
carrying *her* mother's goods,
and as a wife to earn house money.
Now aged, in her daughter's house.
she helps pot each day's product.

She served yogurt every meal: with cereal;
with sharp spices, covering sliced cucumbers;
dressing a salad learned in India; sweetened, with mango
or other fruit as rich dessert; plain.
She gives lessons to women in shelters

and at farmers training sessions, a use
of milk for home and sale, a product
to supplement their lives.

The owners of a resort
in a national park asked her to teach
the chef to make a yogurt palatable
to guests rather than the bitter gruel
of his daily offering. She showed
him care of boiling and long cooling
and with her starter what a fine concoction
came to table. The value of the lesson
was direct, our whole stay written off,
days of viewing remote wild places
and animals, paid for by this mild domestication.

Hive Logs

In orchards and the forest edge
of villages one sees logs hanging.
The length of a man, hollowed, they are the
homes of bees, hung by wire or sisal twine
like a stout scale with nothing in the balance.
The bees work like   bees, producing
deeply flavored honeys from every major
and incidental crop of ordinary
and topical blooms, native and imported.
A beekeeper can never be sure
the flavor his location has induced,
some honeys so spicy and pungent
they taste like exotic sauces.
The wax might be light or almost black.
Often sold as comb to be chewed,
the richer gum tastes balsamic.
Melted and stained, the residue pressed
for all that remains, the wax becomes candles,
wood polish—furniture maker's hands here
are as soft as the finish on their pieces—
and dressing for leathers of animals and birds.

The logs must be split after the bees
have been smoked. Elephant dung
is best, a slow, long, smoky fire
thoroughly stupefying even aggressive species.
Papaya is second best. Honey is so important
such tests have been done.
Wax and honey removed, the logs
fuel sweet-smelling fires
curtailing disease and killing pests.
The logs cost little but the fire costs
the death of the colony after only one season.

To recruit new colonies from the wild
the beekeepers must go farther,
often in parks and tsetse lowlands.

They find or plant Munondo trees, Julbernardi,
globi flora, bee trees with good timber,
and bark for ropes, bins, sacks,
and laxative, plus the food and cure
of the honey itself. New species of bees
are sought and found; new smokers

and hives designed—industry of the man-made
and the natural, with lives in the balance.

The Desert Owl

The half-built house, almost invisible
in the dusk and drought-dust,
   rose on the hill
behind us. Before us,
first at rest, then on the wing,
   headlamp-like eyes tracked us
as we tracked them to a roadside eucalyptus.
Ear tufts, pale streaked breast and back,
a desert owl now in savannah.
My cousin, who has worked in-country
twenty years, the owl and I both visitors,
the tree, Australian gum, huge, were all
imports.

That morning we had raced our jeep along
the old Nairobi-Arusha road.
the wear of cattle feet had ground
the surface flour-fine,
and deep, so as any walkers' feet sunk
out of sight into it
   clouds rose,
together forming a chain of chalky balloons
that dissipated as a rising scrim of tree-high dust.
We had carried with us a mother
   who had appeared at the gate
in the early morning, begging
for a ride for herself
and her hydrocephalic child.
     We had risen before the muezzin
called for early prayers,
to drive as fast as bad roads would allow
toward the hospital and the operation
to install a shunt to save the child

for a desperate life.
As we sped and slowed and sped again
our own dust and that of others
rose from the floorboards,
through the smallest cracks,
stuck to our sweaty skins
and lined our lungs,
lying on even the downcast eyelashes
of the mother who stared
into her child's wide-open eyes.
Arriving home we beheld each other
almost unrecognizable in uniform
head-to-toe uniforms of dusty
coating like fur or down.

In the short, sudden dusk of Equatorial savannah
we looked back at the top of the two-lobed hill,
called locally *Katrina's Bottom*
after a German who lived at the base,
for the day's last glimpse of the house
rising on its perch atop, and were startled
as the turned headlights struck
the eyes and frayed feathers
of the startled owl in recent residence.

A common image half thought
comes into focus clearly—*facade*.
A protruding door nosed between
the two large windows of the house
which seem like huge eyes that look
out on domains less formal.
A year in the making, the house
was half done, and imperfect
from its very beginnings,
shoddy masonry, warped teak timber
from over cut forests, a good design
poorly executed. It would be made comfortable,

pink granite counters, fine wood moldings,
wrought iron window grates
like mullions, not the bars they are.
That is the mask we put on
things to make them homely.
My cousin, his wife, her mother,
will live here, probably
the rest of their lives,
  and the children for a time.

I offered suggestions when asked,
but knew I will always be
a distant correspondent in their lives.

From a nearby village,
from the edge of the village,
I met a man called *Owl*,
because no bird can be the owl's friend.

We found out the baby died
  two days later.
His mother's attempts to raise money
for three weeks
  instead of three days
had cost his life. We had driven her,
but not the baby, home.
Arrangements to be made.

Going home, I flew across the sea ice
south of Greenland,
  space as large and crumpled
in appearance as the vast sands
  the owl often crosses
in its habitat,
  and crossed when flying home
after the long rains came.

I was a short-term refugee by choice
with family to inform me, not hold;
the owl one by privation,
    waiting for what would bloom at home
        to bloom,
    the food for what it feeds on;
both of us with eyes wide open,
     he thinking nothing of it.

Carrying Goats

A hundred Irish dairy goats had arrived
flown into Nairobi, trucked down from Namanga
and dumped without proper papers.
The project leader had to bribe
the border guards for the goats
and his lorry's entry.
He'd been unable to buy water
in that hardest-drought-struck area.
Five goats had died in passage.

People were waiting at the distribution point
and would wait till he arrived.

The lorry man had watered all the goats
when he got to higher springs,
a sort of avalanche of hooves
in the body of the truck,
and drove the hours on.

When the truck hove into view
the women started singing,
a quiet song continued during the passing out
of those good sources of milk and meat.
Patience has few rewards in Africa,
but almost all of those who had been assigned
a goat received an animal.
One woman sang out, "These lovely Irish goats'
feet should not touch the dusty old soil of Africa."
She wrapped her *kanga* around the animal
and began to carry it home. All the women followed
suit, a train of goats carried to large prepared
raised pens where fodder fed they never would
walk the land. These goats will never over-browse

this foreign habitat, or tear it up
with their sharp hooves. The first kids of all the animals
under contract would be passed
to other new contract holders.
Singing into the long day's end,
into the abrupt bright sunset of this middle earth,
a community of owners and those who would be
celebrated a gift they had come,
and would come, to earn, and it was meet.

Orange Benediction

The young widow farmer greeted us
in her dooryard. She was lovely,
thinly dressed in poor cloth
with five young ones active around her.
The bishop we traveled with
put his hand on the youngest boy's head
and said, "When one is young
one really has a very long safari."
The woman had been promised a pregnant heifer
under contract from the diocese.
The one placed with her, bred but not settled,
had died of latent east coast fever.
She now waited for a promised calf
as Passover from one of the heifers
in her village. The bishop's mind
fell to lassitude. "Inertia, We must eliminate
inertia." Her empty, well built
shed stood as testament to readiness.
Her yard was overarched by avocado trees,
the largest orange tree I'd ever seen,
and lemon trees. Fruit, ripe and unripe,
hung heavy and some had fallen
and was falling as we stood.
A garden full of vegetables and hot, hot peppers.
"A husband will appreciate these,"
the bishop told me. "He will adopt
her children and give them his name."
I thought a heifer was needed.

The bishop took up oranges
split them with his knife
and handed them around
before sucking several halves clean.

The juice was cool in the shade.
He asked for a bag. The widow ran
and got a string bag she'd woven.
He gathered oranges and lemons
and encouraged her and the children
to bring him more. Most of us felt one
or two sufficient. "We're helping her
to prevent waste. So generous."

So the old Anglican strode the yard
like down and isle, spewing orange juice
like holy water on all children and adults
in attendance, seeds spit and flying
from his fingers, and they and his frock
covered with the oily essence
from the rind like incense.
He filled his bag and belly
past homily and benediction
and raised both hands to bless and wave
as our car blessedly pulled out and away.

Dying From Lack of Thirst

Maasai boys take the herds out
each day, the men also
if there is a great distance to pasture
or danger near, but often just the boys.
Reports are coming from the villages
to doctors and officials of deaths
amongst the young herders.
They have been found where they rested
under trees or bushes, or collapsed
where they stood doing work
of the world they knew.
They have usually taken sufficient water
with them, or almost enough.
In drought the mothers
and sisters must carry the water pails
far on their heads after waiting
long at the wells. The boys are drinking
only when thirsty, not the amounts
their parents, elders, have taught them.
The wind blows every day, all day.
Even in the heat and drought
the evaporation cools the herders
and they do not know
it is dehydrating them.
So it was in Death Valley as wagon
trains crossed. People and cattle
would collapse. The cooling wind
would belie their need for the water
they carried with them to their places
of death, a deadly economy.

Official warnings go out to the villages:
Tell everyone to drink their true needs.
Train your children better
not to die from lack of thirst.

The Place Where Lions Used to Live

Poles—electric? telephone? aged telegraph?—
run from a remote town to a remoter village,
but no wires run between. Jackson John,
a name self-chosen when his tribe chose
religious self-exile from Kenya,
walks me out two hours
in the mid-day heat to view the village
they are creating in the bush out of the bush.
He pointed toward three ridgelines when we started.
"We will walk beyond the place where lions
used to live, to where we will live."
The main road would be a poor cattle lane
back home. The worn paths are often
from the long walks women and children must make
to carry water kilometers home.
Five-gallon white plastic pails are balanced
laden on even ten-year-olds' heads.
The pails are ubiquitous and handier
than various constructions of the past.
We walk past
four long-haul-truck-sized boulders
jumbled together as if crashed there
atop a high sloped ridge, visible for miles
and giving miles of visibility
where lions used to live. I ask if it was part
of the rush. "Perhaps," Jackson says,
"but they are gone fifteen years now."
"Did the people kill them?"
"There was no need. People killed
all the game. The lions left."
"Where?" "That way we think.
Some game still lives that way."
"Is it taken still?" "*Kimorro.*"

All the wire from the telephone lines,
good copper wire, stolen right after it was hung.
stolen by the poachers to use as snares.
Strong wire for big animals. The meat is sliced
into big pieces, very thin, goat sized,
and dried quickly on hot rocks—
some of the best are the big boulders
where lions used to live—*kimorro*,
bundled up, smuggled across the border.
They pay well there. They are eating our game.
All their game has long been eaten
but they think it is better to eat game.
They may have eaten the lions,
I have heard of such a thing.
No lions live here now."
"Are the people here angry?"
"When there were lions it was very dangerous
but there was game. Our elders remember
the lion killing test. It is everyone's fault.
We wish it back, but raise goats and chickens,
and now cattle. They do not raise these
across the border. Telephones are very useful,
we often need help, families are wide
in the land, but people must eat to talk."

Bitter Cassava

In villages and farmyards across East Africa
the day's cassava is prepared the same.
A woman, or daughter, or son
thumps a large mortar
with a club-sized pestle.
Since the yard-long roots
are full of hydrocyanic juices
a double preparation is required.
The first beating to a crude pulp
in the first mortar removes
the deadlier core. With the outer pulp
poured into a second mortar
not fouled with the poison,
the long thumping comes,
the rise and fall of arms
and heavy pestle
till the starchy pomace is broken fine
like flour. The mouth of the mortar
will finally eat the entire field.
            In other places,
or at other times, as when the Mayans
first used the plant as food,
people have sliced it, pressed it,
heated the pieces, reduced it to flake,
all to reduce the poison.

Proudly, people showed me
whole fields of the shiny shrub
grown as staple. Some small part
is heated on metal plates as flour
and agglomerated into rice-like bits
of tapioca for sale to the West.
The meals I shared of manioc bread

dipped in boiled fish and plantains
made me smile remembering the puddings
of my youth. The youths' work
reminded me of grandmother's tales
of cream separation and the long churning
towards butter, the saleable item
of early dairy. The hard calluses
of the children's hands were the same,
calluses I saw as they, smiling
from well fed faces,
waved in greeting,
and at goodbye.

In some parts of the world
sweet cassava is used, but in most, as here,
bitter cassava grows better, produces more.
In these disparate places, cassava preparation
is part of the rhythm of life
and the *tump* of the pestle
is the metronome timing the seconds
of many of each day's hours of toil.

African Ferries

It rose beside me like a floating basketball court
with high outward facing bleachers.
Though a long dock stood under me,
the captain drove the ferry hard onto the sand.
Several four-wheel-drive vehicles and a stream
of walk-ons boarded first. All passengers climbed
steep outside stairs to long plank seats,
even a mother and son with similarly twisted feet.
The outward sides of their shoes were worn through
and the soles were as when new.
Four single, and two double, long-haul
overland semis trundled down the small
steep slant of beach and up the loading ramp,
great wheels as high as an elephant's eye
for fording what elephants wallow in.
The ferry still had a slight rock from the loading
as it pulled away from the landing
into the hyacinth choked waters
of Lake Victoria's South Sound. Rocks jutted
above the surface, and from my height and angle
I could often see the bottom. Almost across,
one engine quit and we swung in an arc toward
a granite reef, seemed destined to be a tangled
steel island resting in shallow water
on our shallow keel. Engines were reversed in time
and after a time repairs allowed a landing,
another jarring drive onto the strand.

Returning two days later late, we found
trucks backed up a mile, and several hundred people
waiting with their children and bundles.
A steady north wind down the sound
had packed and driven the hyacinth mats

along the shore. The ferry had ground
its motors forward and back and side to side
for two hours trying to make the beach.
No electricity in the village there in the close night
so ferry searchlights and vehicle headlights
lit the passenger audience, as people downed
food and drink from make shift vendors.
Right by the water, and over the water
an astounding number of flies could be seen
in the light. They were thick as breath
and part of it if one breathed hard.
When the ferry finally made it in
at midnight, and loaded, the lights
were shut off for the crossing, the lake-flies so dense.
In that area some people still take wide, round,
long-handled baskets and wave them in a gathering
pattern in the air to collect a thick layer of flies.
The collected mass is formed into cakes
and dried in the sun for later cooking.
As I listened to the engines pound and pound
us through hyacinth islands and angled waves,
I watched the small docking light opposite
slowly get larger, as it seemed every star
in the perfect black dome of sky did also.
Moments of arrival seemed to abound.

Departing for Ukerewe, the largest island
in Victoria, the ferry was small, one large deck
and a small pilothouse on a corrugated roof.
The island was not an island until 1961
when heavy rains and storms cut
the narrow isthmus we passed the remnants of.
Our passage followed days inland
when we had driven around Speke Gulf,
across hills on which Speke stood
to view the waters he had traveled years to see.
The island has the name the lake had then.

The people of these shores often stand
in the water to wash dishes and themselves
and children, to dip irrigation water
to near-shore gardens and fields, to cast
wide nets for shallow-water fish they land
and sort on land. I longed to swim out
from lovely rocks, or to dip my hands
and face in those historic waters,
but bilharzia is endemic so I stayed dry.
The bathers splashing by the dock,
the naked mothers, washing children, pans,
clothes, themselves, will be afflicted
by the blood flukes borne by snails.
Victims suffer, are treated, understand
they cannot separate themselves
from this water without separation
from their lives. As we landed, banks
of thunderstorms rode across the lake,
a ten-thousand-foot scarp of clouds
sun raked, and lit inside and out
by lightning which, against the clouds
 and falling night, left brief bands
of memory-light on the retinae.

The larger ferry south to Mwanza
was built more like a small ship, built
for up to three hundred passengers.
In our three-hour traverse we would pass
the resting place of a ferry twice as large
that had overturned a year before
and, after two days, sank.
Would-be rescuers heard
thumping inside the exposed keel. No diving
equipment available, no holes to be cut,
for the exit of air would have killed
as surely, sunk the ferry more quickly.
Built for six hundred, over eight hundred died;

a hundred survived. Ticket sellers
and ferry operators were charged with murder.
All that explains the crush at the gates
and ticket window. Too many people
to cross on so small a craft. I got a ticket
but wound up climbing up the side
to sail. Others threw their bundles over the rail
and climbed fences and trucks and leaped aboard.
The channel for the first half-hour
lay crooked between bleached-rock protrusions
that looked like small whitecaps breaking for miles.
I stood at the stern. A tuneful phrase,
"It's a long way to Ukerewe," came to mind.
It scanned right and made me think of distance
as time, whether to Tipperary or East Africa.
Later as the captain strolled the deck, he told me
he had sailed the ferry that sank three years,
but had transferred to the longer Kampala route
two months before the sinking. He pointed out
the spot marked with buoys. A tall woman,
as striking as any I'd seen, strode to the rail
and spit in the water there; returned to her group
and pointed; repeated her act.
Crossing that freshwater sea I felt
how any journey can make one feel small,
and grand. The docking and disembarking
at Mwanza was orderly and calm—
women with large, brightly-wrapped bundles
balanced on their heads were given room;
men conversed about singular concerns
in low tones.

Ancient Ironworks

Past Geita, famous for its gold,
or, like how many thousand places,
for its promise of gold,
I note the hillside red
of a more important ore.
Metallurgy came early
to the interlucastrine lands
between Victoria and lakes
of the western Rift,
and here and there remain heaps
and rubble like blackened termite mounds,
the remains of iron smelting furnaces.
With sun-baked bricks
and large coils of clay
the smelters laid up shafts
taller than they
to create a draft strong enough
to melt the ore they loaded in
along with charcoal made from trees
they stripped the savannah for.
Twenty-seven hundred years ago
the Bantu walked from the Grassfields
of Cameroon to dominate huge swaths
of Africa. In tall narrow furnaces
with tuyeres and bellows at the base
they melted the ore
to the concentrated blooms
they pulled from the cooling ashes.
In chaferies formed like bowls
but dug in the earth and lined with clay,
they reheated the ore
to pound out impurities.
Long, iron spearheads,

and sharp tools for the forest and earth
were the means of domination.
Gold, rock crystal and slaves
were traded eastward to the coast.

To many natives now, the remnants,
even from the early parts
of this century, seem another history,
a golden age declined
from those who had the magic
and the knowledge
to the present people who feel
they had no part of it,
who often feel they must cast
off their culture like slag
for the one that rises and retreats
before them like smoke from furnaces
holding the promise of bloom in the ashes.

Swahili Boats

A sailing freighter was drawn up
on the urban beach of lake Victoria.
Heaved far over on its side
with gaping holes in sides and keel,
it lay like a relic there.
A shipwright was measuring planks
for the sawyers who stood on or under
great squared logs sitting
on horses of hardwood cribbing.
The upper man would measure
and saw, and ride the whole apparatus
like a timber mare all day
for days to complete the work.
I recognized the ship's form with a shock
as being almost the same
as carried goods in the first millennium
along the Swahili Corridor.
That trading culture stretched
from present day Somalia
to Mozambique. Their ivory, gold,
fine rock crystal, timber and slaves
were resold by their Arab partners
into China, India, Iran, Sicily,
Moorish Spain. It was *mtepe*
much like the one I watched repaired
that could most easily sail
the difficult seas, shallow reefs,
and treacherous isles of that coast. Those ships
and those Swahili traders carried
the goods north to the deep-sea
going dhows.

The shipwright had purchased
mringa-mringa, a rare and fine hardwood
like teak. Such timbers had roofed
the Sultan's palace in Bagdad
and the finest houses.
Traded African slaves had drained
the great swamps of Shatt-Al-Arab
before they rose in revolt
in 960. Ambergris
and ivory had reached China,
and fine glazed pottery had come back
to grace homes now found in diggings
recovering a past lost to history.

Other obscure patterns
may have been set off.
Gypsies moved west from India
through the Middle East
into Europe. Their carving of quartz,
goldsmithing, ivory jewelry,
was much in demand,
could have driven them or drawn them
to migrate with the trade.
The trade carried knowledge with it
and helped begin the end of dark times.
The shipwright knows nothing of this.
his ships are built to the design
he learned. I watched him drive
caulking cord deep into the seams.
He said at these distances
the wind is still best, but to make money
the owners take chances
with the sailor's lives, and his ships
are stressed. He sees them sail,
as do I, too heavily laden,

only inches of freeboard,
decks awash in fairly calm waters
as the ships come into ports for nights
just as they must have
when coasting in their first expression.

Canyonlands

The canyons are hundreds of feet deep,
vertical rock and earthen cliffs
stand as testament to a dry climate,
constant moisture rounds its world.
Brilliant yellow strata lie atop
a variety of reds from deepest blood
to palest sunset, a landscape echoed
in itself. A kind of blue is low
but not in shadow, perhaps clay
or shaley outcrop, then black,
shadow and impermeable base rock together.

Heading for farms high in the hills,
we rode the canyon rim for miles
and saw no other tourists
at what could be a Mecca,
the gorge itself and, in remnant pools,
glossy ibis, sacred ibis, haddada ibis—
the purples, black, white, and greens,
a bloom of birds—jacanas, Egyptian geese,
herons, black storks, crowned cranes,
hamerkops. The last called *king of birds*
because its huge nest is used by so many others,
even eagles, and thus are thought to serve it.
The swirl of startled flight against the strata
outdoes the brightest parade
down a skyscrapered street.

The ride was to a celebration for a local man
receiving the golden farmer award.
His highland people, the villages, cleared
the forests from the hills,

resulting in cascades in heavy rains
sent ripping down the shallow valleys,
and in two decades gorges formed
that it seems might take millennia.

We ravage landscape
and are ravaged by it,
its forms, embedded in our minds,
recognizable and beyond
recognizing.
Not far from that place
landscape was first imprinted
on what could be called
a human mind, the grassed and treed savannah,
what might be drawn if anyone was asked
to draw the ideal landscape.
Many of us are drawn to it from colder,
harder, wetter, drier climes
we also love.

The farmer had helped lay out
and build miles of contours
on the slopes to catch the rain
for crops and to stop erosion,
which was eroding the people's
ability to live. The game is gone.
The crops were green in deep drought
and forest birds still lingered
in those village trees
and in those trees grown thick for fodder,
leguminous leucaena and sesbania; mulberry
with leaves for cattle, fruit for humans.
On new contours the pigeon pea
held the soil till heavier roots would grab in
and feed the people as well.
The soil is better now, as is the water

from the slowing of it,
but what was lost below
is long past reclamation.

A man accosted me
as I glassed the birds.
"Why do you care more for the birds
than humans?" "I do not.
In my state of Vermont
we also cleared the forests.
Many animals became extinct.
Wicked floods wrecked the railroads,
washed villages away, killed many.
The forests have regrown,
some of the animals were reintroduced,
but the birds were always there.
We later poisoned many, but have stopped.
It seems to me nothing is too far gone
if the birds remain. Your farmers are planting
many trees. The village is healthy,
and the birds, too, it seems."
"Thank you for telling me this."

Once again what started as description
had become story, images to an end
which is not possible to tell,
but carried forward on every eroding
or alluvial current.

The Second Wife

My cousin and I stood in the farmer's yard
by his *banda*, half shed, half corral,
where the cow my cousin arranged
for him to receive stood.
The farmer's wife brought sliced oranges
and limes from their orchard.
A slice of Lake Victoria shimmered beyond
a nearby hill which appeared to move
in the sour heat of February summer.
The farmer told of his children,
how the money from the milk
sent them to school,
paid for the house,
and none now lived there.
A large woman in a striped *kanga*
draped as dress and another wrapped
formally around her head
strode across the drive
and tried to dismiss the wife
from the courtyard, and started
animated talks with the farmer.
It seems she was a second wife
to a first wife now long dead.
She and the farmer own the cow
together but by agreement
all care was given over
to him to raise their children.
The split occurred when he took
a second second wife who was not like
a daughter to the now first wife,
which is tradition, but was more like
her sister in age and temperament,
and no by-your-leave of the first

was asked. the second wife had borne
a child, and money for its raising
now lay in limbo since it had not
been blessed by the first wife. The child
was playing in the yard with avocado
seeds whose fruit dropped randomly
around us as we talked.
                              The first wife
held the contract, and a position
as head of the farmers' cooperative.
The farmer bowed his head a little
as they talked. The second wife picked up
her child and stood by the farmer.
The first wife did not look.
My cousin said, "The farmer wants
the first wife back, but will not ask."
The cow was heavy with calf,
and its two dry months had been hard.
The first wife was both delegate
and delegation—odd for such
power to be so closely removed.
Large dust-devils swirled
like motives in the yard.
                    The grass widow
looked at the young wife's child
from the corner of her eye
as one might view an item
at an auction one was tempted to bid on.
The farmer held one hand heavily
on the neck of the cow, who chewed
on the hand-chopped feed, contented
amidst its creation.

White Bats

A woman was preparing lunch
in a house in the hills above
the Serengeti plain. The breeze outside
had kept the flies at bay
but inside they were relentless.
"The mosquitoes will be dreadful
at dusk. Are you on chloroquine?"
"Something, yes." Because resistant
strains have become endemic.
I watched a small white bat flutter
to her ceiling, the underside of thatch.
The bat was almost hairless,
its body the size of my thumb
and it carried two young.
"Are they helpful?" I pointed.
"They eat many mosquitoes,
and I like them, but we kill them
when too many nest. Guano
in the kitchen is even more unpleasant
than bugs. Some locals fear them."
I mentioned the bat boxes people use back home.
She, nor I, knew if they would work there.
She said she might try,
pleasant nod to a nosy stranger,
and what would be the draw
over the open airy, beam and thatchwork
of her house, even the geckos freely shifted
from the outside to the inside walls
depending on time of day and heat.
Settled for the afternoon, wing-wrapped,
the bat looked like a chrysalis,
the fact and phantom of itself
born anew each late day.

Omunya

"Can't be cut," my guide translates.
Red berries on a smothering vine
covering shrubs in a severe drought.
"When the women bundle sticks,
they use this vine. No matter how they pull
it will not break." He does not know
if it is poison, but no birds we see
are eating the only fruit I see.
Jackson John—his English name—
has walked me over dry hills
to see what will become the *shamba,*
the village center. Communal crops
will grow in the large cleared fields,
where a school is rising from the salty earth,
so salty deep footings must be dug
and filled with crushed rock. Actually broken rock,
women crack boulders
with fire, on which to pour
the concrete foundations then safe from corrosion.
I tell him of deep footings in my land
to reach below the frost line.
We are both impressed.
He asks what my land is like.
"At this time of year two feet of snow
cover everything except thick forests
of bare trees. The lakes are frozen over;
fishermen drive their cars and trucks
out on the ice to cut holes and fish."
"We have heard such things.
We believed they were stories."
A wide circuit leads us past the new well
dug by an aid society.
Tracks spoke away from it

in a great wheel of thirst.
Women and children stand
for hours to pump their necessary share
to cart kilometers home
in buckets and tubs balanced on heads
and necks strained by the load.
The well is locked each Sunday.
This is Sunday. We pass three women
in a ditch where a seep slowly fills
a hand held pan, four minutes a quart.
They have filled two five-gallon pails,
will finish with three, a morning gone.
They ask Jackson John in their tongue
what he is doing with me.
He describes our small journey, he tells me.
"How do you speak with him?"
"My English is good."
Then in a tone I cannot tell
if it is banter or mean,
intonation lost in translation,
they say, "Why do you not change
your skin and become English?"
His retort is light but pointed.
They wave him off and we wave and go.
We walk through offshoots
of the Rift Valley, up to higher ground
and back down slopes to the bottoms
where firewood and the vine
are more common. I search the earth
for a fossil, bone, skull, or a tooth
which might hold at its core
DNA that unraveled and raveled
cut itself and mutated
so he and I are what we see
and random chance has brought us here,
but our genes remained
virtually interchangeable.

even more so the DNA of our mitochondria,
passed from mother to child
a*d initium, ad infinitum,*
Across the years and continents,
one unbroken string of possibility
and origin—*omunya.*

Shoveling Fish

Mouth brooders
descended from a vast family of Lake Tanganyika,
the hugely deep lake of the Great Rift,
spread to lakes Nyassa and Victoria.
Fish still found in the latter only in certain bays or on shallow reefs,
fish of aquaculture—ponds dug since ancient Egypt—
small as a flattened thumb,
fish shoveled into grain sacks to feed the war-injured and refugees
of the many rifts between peoples. Heaps of silver fish the size of
    thumbs
flattened and dried so each heap that fills the shovel blade to the
    socket and frog
looks like shredded patterned tin foil
or ancient thinly minted coins of the Swahili
for their trade with Europe in the first millennium.
I use the same style aluminum scoop
the color of the fish to shovel snow at home.

Perch over a hundred pounds are often caught in the wide waters of
    Victoria.
Hundreds of varieties of cichlids have been extirpated
by the introduced Nile Perch.
Motor boats pitch in waves as they tow small sailboats
to be released in turn like dories on the Grand Banks,
each skipper-fisherman's task to fill his small hold.
Stories abound of perch rising to key chains
dangling from belts or pants loops
and taking them like spinning lures or spoons
and pulling the men overboard into the realm of the sought.
The forests of Mwanza have been stripped
for fires to dry the great bodies of the perch.
The rows and rows of fish flakes on the shore
by the reedy harbor are now much less used

the perch have so diminished other stocks.
The dried perch, the size and shape of large flat stones
are piled in perfect squares on large pallets
so it looks as if the foundations for great buildings
to come are being laid. The would-be city of fish,
streets not paved or cobblestoned
but plated, gilded, with scales that stick
to everything, but eventually dry and drift
in the wind like shed wings of termite hoards.
Fish not already dedicated or sold
are mongered from flats and corners
of the city rising along these aisles and alleys
filled with the smoke of drying,
damped with the oil pressed from the fish flesh.

From here fresh fish are also marketed,
tilapia for the homes and restaurants of Mwanza and environs,
tilapia shipped in the hold of Air France jets all over the world.

All this is written in the present tense not to make the past immediate,
but because it all continues.
People stand in the bags to pack them,
their feet glisten with fish oil, then a bundle of straw
is placed as seal and protection before the mouth of each sack
is hand sewn closed with twine and heavy needle.
Pallets of dried perch neatly stacked in concentric tiers.
The perch look the shape and size of throw rugs.
The simple drying racks of sun-bleached wood,
which line the shore east of the great open market
and shipping point, do not suffice to dry their large bulk.
Deforestation to dry the hundred, and more, pound deep wide bodies
has stripped inhabited steep rocky outcrops of shade and holding
    roots.
Sewage flows unchecked, as do the heavy rains of fall.
So timber and harvest, erosion and crops,
the lake and those living in and around it
all fall victim to the one introduced species' omnivorous maw.

And if pain could be measured in fish,
if each represented only a moment,
the mountains, hills, cities are made of fish,

but if each small silver body was a release,
was a flimsy coin, the tin-foil-like coins of the Swahili Corridor
unearthed in digs on the long, distant, ocean shore, purchasing
a second of succor
for each survivor, that too is immeasurable.

The bags are filled, tied, carted away.
The pallets like modular buildings are loaded
on trucks headed on good roads and war-torn tracks
to the east where refugees stream and hide.

The tarpaulins are piled high with freshly pressed fish,
the cornerfish of pallets are newly laid for course after course.

Termites

The wind blew off the Serengeti.
I sat in church, listened to lovely
response-singing, male and female
voices by turn and together
after the minister spoke,
and after each member
who rose to witness.
The wind whined like the sirens
of the International Tribunal
in the city we had left behind.

The wind blew harder off the Serengeti
and lifted the roof right up,
after a woman had stood
and praised the Lord
for sparing her child in the night,
for keeping the beams of the falling house
from crushing her daughter.
The church was so termite riddled
that we could suddenly see vistas
through the walls, and the roof
rose clear of almost every upright.

And the wind that lifted the roof up
and shook the walls hard, dropped
pounds of dust on all of us.
Women dressed in white went grey.
An old man bearing faith and himself
had walked many miles to speak.
The dusty rose of his headband faded;
his feet that looked like braided leather
hardly shifted in his sandals smoothed

by wet and wear to a gloss nothing
in that place had.

The wind made the whole place
shudder and shift but left it standing.
I did not share their praise.
Did He adjust each termite's meals
so over time each of millions took
enough and left enough for the result
that managed to stand above us?
Or did constant tabulation
or last minute calculations add up
the damage and send a wind
only strong enough to shake not fell?
Or at the moment of racking
was notice suddenly given
and the building compelled to stand no matter?

Were I to believe as they believe
I would wish a constant accounting,
an awareness of how things might fall
and when, but that would grant
that things are also allowed to fall,
and who to praise for the descent
of beams and roofs, or for the fall
of Hutu machetes, clubs, and axes
on their Tutsi neighbors.

An Umber Sky

Circling the airport in dangerous winds,
we see the huge whitewashed greenhouses
on the shoulders of Mount Meru
where the light and climate are right
for the European cut-flower trade.
The light is not right this day,
the whitewashed glass is yellowed,
as though lit with weak incandescence,
and the surface of the world seems blurred.

Roughly grounded in our landing,
the plane jostled even in its runout taxi,
we see dust devils towering
like great smokestacks and smoke plumes
doing the work of picking up
the crust and dust the drought created
and turning it into umber sky,
no part of which is blue,
no part of which is not dry.

Though not tornadoes, if the twisters strike
dead on they will lay
termite riddled buildings low
and tear the spindly, tree-trunk scaffolding
off the upper stories of concrete buildings
being poured. The entire population
breathes its own landscape,
smells the soil it has compacted
and stripped of cover,
and sees its richness roil the sky
 now painted raw and burnt.

Training Sessions

Eight years ago Sabeyo had been picking potatoes
from the road. Two weeks before that he had planted
eleven bags of Irish potatoes in soil slash-cleared
by him and others all the way up his home-side hill
to the, by law, altitude protected topknot forest.
That silly remnant could not absorb or slow the fall
of fallen rain down those steep slopes.
His potato hills had washed onto and down
the gullied road. In a mile he retrieved one bag.

He holds a thin arm up on this day of my visit as if to show.
"...a burlap sack of potatoes that were not good
to plant or eat. We ate them."

My cousin had found him the next day laying out
crude contours. My cousin told him if he would take
husbandry and conservation training he would receive
a pregnant heifer and agency contract.
Where his potatoes and hopes washed and rotted,
today the hill is heavily vegetated on contours
which can withstand the long and heavy rains
of monsoon. Tree lucerne and Gliricidia grow tall
and shade maize and peas and fodder grasses,
as well as carrots, yams, and beans on contours
narrowed by the pitch of land.
He must boil tree lucerne seeds, but it is good
in cold and altitude. The other tree will grow
from cuttings easily, and both hold his land well.
"Contours without trees are nothing," he says.
He shows me his silage pit lined with banana leaves
which keep moisture out. He has a cistern-like pit
for producing methane. We stand in his narrow pen
for tick spraying and injection of the animals

against various and multiple disease.
He has expanded his house, it has a fine white
exterior covered in flowering vines. Vines also shade
his outdoor meeting room where farmers come
for training. At first they would not come.
He aided some. He punctured the bloat-swollen
rumens of cows, the canula releasing the foamy gases
when it was too late for anything else. He showed neighbors
how corn and sorghum stover, sugar cane tops,
and any straws, could be used for feed if fermented
three weeks using water and urea. They saw his cared-for
cattle out-live, and out-produce, theirs. He passed
five calves on under new contracts. Three hundred farmers
have been through his training now, and most have flourished.
"What is most important," he says, "Erwin promised me
a cow. And I got one."

Baobab Fruit

Cracking the heavy husks
was like feeling the bone
beneath the short rough fur
of some long-skulled beast
proving difficult to kill
with stone age implements.
Having bludgeoned open the shuck
my nephews and I extracted long pieces of the nutmeat.
Such exertions in the drenching heat
on the beach south of Mombasa
both magnified and minimized the prize,
pulp with the taste of cream of tartar,
acidic chunks dissolving powdery,
and coating the tongue.

Bush babies had cried their child-like
cries the night before in those trees
whose nuts we ransacked.
We had tried to spot them with flashlights
as we circled the trees as big around
as an African house, thick bark
the feel and color of elephant or rhino skin.
Vervets raced through the crowns
by day to reach fig and mangrove trees
drooping with overripe fruit by the shore.
Fox bats looped in and around
those laden trees through every dusk,
and hung in them and the baobab by day.
Inland, a herd of hungry elephants
will dismantle a baobab tree
to eat its moist, pithy wood
as easily as we cracked apart its fruit.
Native peoples honor the tree,

but its appearance upset the Arabs
when they first reached this far south
they said it had its roots in the air,
the devil's work. I sat in massive shade
beside its barrel trunk, a hogshead trunk,
a great tun, sucking the mucilaginous fruit pulp.
I thought of mother's pies and candies,
the cream of tartar used to make them,
and of my fingers powdery with that spice
which is not a spice but the lees,
the dregs of fermentation,
used to other ends; and of the ends of the world
traveled to, discovered, for the world's rough
and subtle flavors.

Arusha Art Alley

Early morning the doors
of closet-sized shops swing open
in the alley off Clock Tower Square,
exactly half way on the Cape to Cairo highway.
The art, mostly ebony carvings of animals,
stands in rows as if herds
lining a riverbank to drink
in the torpor of an African day
amidst a drought, time of accommodation.
The dealers stand, waiting for walkers,
wanting to show them also the beads
and intricate barrettes, the plates, bowls,
and platters of imagined exotic meals.
Here and there an odd beast,
a pure blue cheetah, a rhinoceros splashed
with red and purple, a knife-horned oryx,
a carefully painted eastern pale chanting goshawk,
no telling whether an image
of wild-caught passager or haggard,
but tightly jessed.
A child has shaped, and let sun dry
in the sun-baked street,
animals from poachy soil
where often illegal hunters, poachers,
quietly stab, poach, instead of shoot
the animals that with domestic herds
trample and pock the earth, or poach it.
And here in the alley the carver's objects,
each standing in the stead of the living
as directly and various as a word,
testify to what a fine poaching art is.

Doctor Sokombi

A barefoot doctor program had saved his life.
His missionary father and helpmate wife
had returned to their island home,
after selling their goods and mainland home,
when the father quit his government job.
    The bible, seed and loam
of his life, had grown too large to ignore.
He sold his English car,
a thousand shillings returned from six,
renounced his membership of the bar,
judging his life judged and wanting,
and sailed over Nyanza Victoria's rocky deeps
to preach to his people and start his family.
The Sea of Galilee keeps
recurring in his writings and sermons
of that time, even the one of the lost
son, skin blue as deep water.
Lips only slightly embossed
on that sheet of a face were kissed
to both warm and open for the insufflation,
then clearing, then more breath
until finally the para-physician
had brought the child back from death.

His father taught Emmanuel as much
as might befit a boy of learned parents
and sent him to the village school,
and found and scrounged tuition
for him to go to the international school
in Mwanza, across the sound.
The boy also fished to earn his fees,
and shipped on sailing freighters overloaded
so waves lapped over the low freeboards

constantly. The boats put into small ports or bays
at night so as not to go down in darkness
on routes north to Musaka, Jinja, and Kisumu.
Exposure to the water gave him bilharzia
often, and bouts of malaria inured him
to worry about it, or to visitors' worries.
The boy sailed his own small craft to school
each Sunday and home each Friday afternoon
across that freshwater sea, receiving
more education than most from his city,
and it wasn't enough.

Cold War alliances allowed him to leave
his family, village, and land
to study in the cold climate of Moldovia.
He received his degree and advanced degree
in animal science. He traveled the Eastern Bloc,
Berlin in spring; Prague and Sofia,
cities on great rivers; hiked the Olympic
mountains of Yugoslavia. Those glories
were not enough to make him ever regret
returning home, but he would pass around
pictures of the time like a jeweler
showing his most precious stones
to only those who understood value.

When he drove up to the hospital
to show that gift to the city,
handsome Bauhaus pile on top
of one of the seven hills,
he found his aunt sitting like a stone
on a stone, her daily home
for two months, waiting her daughter.
"Tuberculosis," she said, "the doctors
say they may release her soon."
"I had not seen her for half a year,"
Sokombi told me later. "Doctors

tell family such things to keep
them from knowing, being too afraid
to help a member with AIDS." Families
of many, many children alone,
were camped out about the grounds,
mats and tents and twig-built lean-tos
staked out abodes of some duration.
Smoke drifted from cooking fires
fed wood from denuded hills.
He offered his aunt money and comfort
and prayer, and it was not enough.

He parceled out a shipment of cattle
that had come from Namanga
north through Kenya because the Serengeti
was too dry. The cattle were still
drought stricken, and one had a bent neck
from the crush and rough travel.
The would-be dairy-men and -women
were reluctant to take ill looking cattle
though they were healthy
and would recover, even the injured
beast held valuable genes.
But Sokombi wouldn't force the contract.
He found a man on the edge of the city
who had enough room for an enclosure,
though not enough to grow the fodder required,
but his neighbors would help him
to cut and carry and chop garden
and leguminous tree waste for feed
in return for milk, and yogurt, and cheese,
and contract calves.

Late one afternoon we drove to his brother's.
His sister-in-law greeted us alone,
perhaps her husband would be home late.
Late, we drove through the large town

lit here and there by oil lamps and beeswax candles.
We had eaten chupatties in a dim café,
relieved ourselves by squatting
on the boards over a deep open pit,
a common latrine, and arrived full
and sleepy. She had prepared a meal,
slaughtered for a great meal,
on the thin supposition that we and her husband
would come in time. We ate the chicken,
and of the goat, but not enough,
we could not do it justice. She asked Sokombi
in Swahili if it was not presented right.
We tried to make amends through our apologies,
we said we had not done proper honor
to so fine a meal. Her most-lovely-face-
I-saw-in-all-of-the-Africa-I-saw face smiled
such as a saint might smile,
but at one who has done a grievous thing.

And when, deep in the bush,
I fainted from an infection,
he told my cousin I was breathing
when my cousin had collapsed
beside me with a cry of "Oh. No."
A woman brought her sleeping mat
out into the compound.
I slept soundly the several hours
they went deeper in-country
to inspect herds and farms.
He brought me powdered glucose,
bananas, and later pineapple
from a bicycle vendor trundling
his wide load to market.
Felt it wasn't enough,
that I wasn't well enough,
that we should return me to hospital
rather than sail over the waters

to his island home. Bless the power
of the antibiotics I carried,
I felt we could travel, that he could show
us his family, and wonders,
Ukerewe's hills covered with mango trees
in size and shape and number
like the sugar maples back home.

He introduced me to his mother and father,
their small house and compound.
They brought out pictures of themselves
when young, and of Sokombi,
and there was the car. We had seen
the car with original plates
minus its steering wheel to keep it safe
on the streets of Mwanza,
its inflationary value a thousand times
six thousand. The coins his parents had hoarded
for old age, bright well-struck coins
with a hole in the middle
were now worth less than the metal.
Laws had been passed to keep people
from using them as roofing washers,
the wealth of a lifetime
holding down rusty corrugated steel.
I heard no complaints
and all through our visit they beamed.

Because the island maintown was the birthplace
of President Nyere, the streets are paved
and residents hoped for electricity
to come from the mainland soon,
though his death had left their pull elastic.
Sokombi showed us lake-side gardens
flooded each morning from the snail-infested
waters of the reedy shallows.
Rising early I once walked to a jetty

where I found crowds bathing,
women one side men on the other,
and quickly retreated. A huge Nile crocodile
tail-slapped the slats of his large crib,
a would-be attraction for small change.
A woman ran after us to give my cousin
seeds from the drumstick tree we had stopped
to admire. We admired the squash and gourds
of a man surprised at our wish to talk
of his common labors and common crop.
We gave a roadside beggar the change
from our pockets, little enough
but he was surprised at the small rain.

In the yard of a richer man
we studied his *banda*, which he had built
quickly to qualify for a cow. Complaints
had been raised that he didn't deserve
a contract based on speed.
"Of all the ill-built *bandas* I have seen,"
said Sokombi, "this is the most ill-built."
The water tank could be fouled with feed
and dung; the concrete floor wouldn't drain
the slurry; the required roof was not placed
to protect the cow from sun or driving rain.
Sokombi would make him build again,
he could keep the cow, but rules
for eligibility were changed.
No ruling out disease, but trying to rule
contagion, we went where rinderpest
had flared and a hundred thousand cattle
were receiving vaccine. Huge numbers
were saved, but many had lost
animals and livelihood, and we heard
that cases of heartwater and blackquarter
were breaking out to the south.
We would be heading south in the morning.

And he, and you reader, thought it was all set
long ago in disappointment, that nothing
would be enough,
could be enough,

                    but for many he met
what he offered was just what they needed,
more than they'd known could be had.